Thank for ::
heart and
for others

Sean!

Well-Intentioned People Say DUMB Things:

Practical advice for comforting those who are grieving

L. Keith Taylor

Well-Intentioned People Say **DUMB** Things:

Practical advice for comforting those who are grieving

ISBN 978-1-387-34777-3

Published by L. Keith Taylor

Printed by Lulu.com

Endorsements

When my husband died, my life fell apart. Not only was I dealing with extremely overwhelming grief but also my children's grief. This book will provide insights into understanding the finality of death and other's reaction to your grief. Dr. Taylor's honesty and compassion showed me how to embrace life again; how to continue to grow with my children; how to cherish what I had; how to keep my husband's memories alive and above all continue to live a life filled with love.

Emily Campoli
Widow

Keith, I sincerely thank you for composing this guide for people whose desire is to offer words of comfort during times of deep sadness, grief and loss. Your words of wisdom come from decades of experience in offering personal support to others, teaching and leading grief support groups and teaching facilitator-training groups. So often as a spiritual care provider in an acute care hospital I hear the words such as, "I want to visit my dying friend, but I don't know what to say or what to do." May this book provide inspiration, comfort and hope.

Rev. Vicki Cousins
Coordinator, Spiritual Care,
Southlake Regional Centre,
Newmarket, ON

The reality of death is that it can come alongside us in an instant. In other cases it courts us for a while and then enjoins itself to us. Nobody escapes it; nobody is getting out of here without experiencing it. Therefore, its subject matter is so very important. Dr. Taylor has many years of experience, both as one having to deal with loss on a personal level and as one who offers solace to those in the turmoil of bereavement. He speaks the truth in love, he confronts the reality with precision and is careful, oh so careful in what he says and how he speaks. He does not apologize for death, he does not make any excuses for its invasion, but in a refreshing and buoyant approach to the topic, he helps us navigate our way through the most difficult time of one's life. Thank you, Keith.

Dr. Ian Fitzpatrick
National Director, Church of the Nazarene,
Former District Superintendent, Ontario and Quebec

After the death of our teenage son, we were completely lost. Our weekly counselling sessions with Keith were a constant in a world of chaos. Knowing that we had Keith to talk to each week gave us the strength to get through this incredibly difficult time. His words of wisdom and direction continue to help us navigate our grief journey.

Dale and Brenda Leeper
Parents

If you want to help a person with his or her grief please read this book for practical advice. You will learn about this very complex, soul-crushing, personal experience called grief. I became a widow and single mother of two young children after my husband had a cardiac arrest beside me in a remote cottage setting. It shook me to the core for a very long time; I was drowning in grief. The 'tsunami' turned into waves of grief, lessening as the years passed by. Yes, I still have these waves of grief after ten years but they are gentler now and I have learned to manage them. THIS IS NORMAL! Thank you to Dr. Keith Taylor for being the lifeboat in my time of need. Your knowledge on this subject along with your compassionate listening and guidance helped me tremendously.

Kelly Magner, RN

Oh that all the *well-intentioned* people I encountered following the death of my infant son were as perceptive, knowledgeable and compassionate as Dr. Keith Taylor. Luckily, I was both privileged and blessed to have him accompany me on my journey through the wilderness of grief. It is my hope that all who read this book will be similarly enlightened and comforted, both mourners and *well-intentioned* people alike.

Laura Morrison-Flint,
Content Editor, National Post/Postmedia.
Facilitator, Grief Support Group

I've known Dr. Keith Taylor for the entirety of my medical career. At this juncture that amounts to twenty-two years. At first he and I were colleagues; over time I'm honored to say that we've become friends. We have always shared a desire to comfort and care for people in the throes of different stages of death and grief. I know him to be a man of very practical compassion. With an evolving yet always delicate balance of empathy and realism, Keith has devoted his life to somehow accompanying those who feel completely deserted through death, and to consoling those who are understandably inconsolable through the deepest of losses. In this vitally important book, he provides guidance to care-providers, clergy, relatives, friends, acquaintances, co-workers and others who are called upon to comfort the grieving among us. Keith deftly offers insight as to how we so often unwittingly make things worse through ill-chosen words and misdirected expressions. We all make these *well-intentioned* blunders. And with this newfound insight we can all do a better job of comforting the bereft.

Barry Nathanson, B.A., M.D., M.H.C.M., FRCPC, FACP,
Adjunct Lecturer, Faculty of Medicine,
University of Toronto,
Chief of Staff, Stevenson Memorial Hospital,
Alliston, ON

Dr. Taylor has done extensive work in the field of grief and bereavement and has significantly assisted those working along their grief journey. Any individual who has suffered a loss will do well to read this book.

Wes Playter - Funeral Director & Manager
Roadhouse & Rose Funeral Home
Newmarket, ON

When our daughter Lisa was killed in a car accident at the age of seventeen, we were completely lost. Our whole life was turned upside down in a blink of an eye and the grief we felt was overwhelming. As we had another daughter remaining, drowning in our sorrow wasn't an option. When we met with Keith, he was understanding and compassionate without judging. It took time and work on our part but with Keith's help and guidance my husband and I were able to navigate through this most difficult time.

Cheryl and Mike Thivierge, Parents

Keith, thank you for sharing a perspective that we all miss, unless we are grieving or have grieved the loss of a loved one. Even then, those feelings are so fragile and personal they cannot be imagined or understood by anyone but the person who is experiencing them. Your insights will help us to think about what we say or do so that we accomplish what we genuinely intend, often in very difficult circumstances.

Tony Van Bynen
Mayor, Town of Newmarket, ON

I first met Dr. Keith Taylor, while he was teaching a course on Disenfranchised Grief. It was there that his story and mine intersected. We've become good friends. I was deeply grateful that he accepted an invitation to speak to our congregation and community about grief and shared his understanding of some of the helpful and non-helpful things people say to those experiencing the death of a loved one. With gentle courage and grace he encouraged me to begin our own grief support group. After each email his valediction says, "SOAR," which constantly gave me the affirmation to continue in the endeavour to support the many who grieve the loss of dear loved ones and encourage them to re-make their lives. Keith is compassionate, and deeply honours those who mourn and grieve. This book is a vital, practical and highly compassionate contribution as we learn to companion alongside people experiencing grief and loss. Thank you, Keith!

Winnie Visser, M.Div., RP, RMFT
Congregational Care Coordinator, Fellowship CRC
Brighton, ON

Dedication

For over twenty-seven years, I have had the privilege and honour to work with those who were preparing to say good-bye to loved ones. I have helped make funeral arrangements, conducted funeral services and walked with people on their personal grief journeys. Their hearts are bruised. Their pain is deep. Their wounds are life altering. And still, they reach out and invite others to listen to their stories. One must hold their hearts tenderly and compassionately while listening with an open heart that does not judge or evaluate.

This book is dedicated to you who have invited me into your mourning. This is **YOUR** book – **YOUR** voice – **YOUR** journey. I trust that you know you have been heard and in being heard you have felt encouraged and supported.

L. Keith Taylor

Contents

The feeling within you of being understood can heal more
wounds than any medication or kind words
or bits of advice.

Hallowell & Ratey, 1994

Acknowledgements

I once heard that, "It takes a village to raise a child." Throughout the writing of this book, it became obvious it takes more than one to write a book.

My heart-felt thanks to:

- **my sister, Gail**, who spent countless hours editing, re-writing, asking too many questions, commenting on content and critiquing harshly (I am convinced she thoroughly enjoyed it!). Her willingness to journey with, support and encourage me is greatly appreciated;

- **my administrative assistant, Joan**, who went beyond her job description in the preparation of the manuscript;

- **Laura** for the cover design of the book and for her encouragement;

- **the hundreds of people** whose voices resound throughout this book. Thanks for giving me permission to share your stories. You have been and continue to be an immense encouragement;

- **my church family,** who have walked with me on this journey and for your partnership, support, notes of encouragement and allowing me the time to write, I do not take for granted;

- **many others**, too numerous to mention. Your encouragement has helped me to persevere and keep writing. (A special word to those who bought a photocopy of the cover and have waited and waited for the pages between the covers to be written. Thanks for hanging in and not asking for your money back.);

- **my financial supporters**, who have asked to remain anonymous. Your encouragement and generosity is overwhelmingly appreciated;

- **my Dad**, who in the last year of his life, kept encouraging me to finish the book. Sadly, he died before it was completed;

- **my good friend Dr. Les Galicinski**, for his invaluable computer skills in formatting.

- **my wife, Pamela**. I have been talking about this book for years. I needed the final push to "get it done" or "cease talking about it!" Her faithful support has made the journey well worth the walk.

Preface

My grief journey

My first experience with grief occurred at the age of fourteen when my Mom died after a four-year remission from cancer. I've been told I was very close to my Mom but despite having little memory of her as a person, I do have life-altering memories that surround her funeral.

For instance, I recall that I chose not to show any emotion at my Mom's funeral and graveside service. Although I saw other mourners crying, I wasn't crying and wouldn't cry! I remember thinking, "This was MY Mom! Death is wrong!" Inwardly, I was seething with anger, resentment and bitterness. Above all, I questioned a God who I believed, up to this point, was a God of love. For me, death became an enemy.

Another vivid memory transports me to the receiving line after the funeral where my family and I received condolences from *well-intentioned* people. Unfortunately, their condolences just compounded my pain. I struggled with hearing words such as: "At least she did not suffer too long," or "Remember God will not give you more than you can handle," or " If there is anything you need, just call," or "God must have needed her." One statement that deeply impacted me was, "I know how you feel." I wondered how someone, whose mother was still living, could know how I was feeling? And even if that person's mother was living, how could they really know how I was really feeling?

My second encounter with deep grief occurred ten years later with the death of my stepmother (a woman who never aspired to replace my Mom, but who became a beloved friend). Once again, I found myself standing beside an open grave, receiving the condolences of *well-intentioned* people. Again, I heard words that inflicted deep wounds: "How wonderful that you and your family had her for ten years," or "Let's be thankful God brought her into your life when she was most needed by you and your sister," or "How fortunate that your Dad had fallen in love with two wonderful women. He must feel truly blessed."

Despite the hurt and confusion those words brought, I knew they were spoken by *well-intentioned* people in an effort to comfort, encourage and assist. However, to this day, those words and similar words offered to those whom I have counselled for over twenty years are haunting. 'Wonderful,' 'blessed' and 'thankful' do not seem to fit when standing over a grave. I am reminded often that a great chasm exists between the condolences offered by *well-intentioned* people and those who are receiving those words and whose hearts are breaking. Sadly, even today, grieving people continue to be faced with the constant challenge of hearing condolences that are meant to provide support but instead cause hurt.

Note to Reader

Greetings Dear Friend!

This book reflects the grief journeys of hundreds of people with whom I have worked over the years. Who better to help us understand how to comfort and support than those on this journey? In an effort to honour and reflect the experiences of these people and in preparation for writing this book, I asked these folks to respond to the following questions:

- 🌳 Tell me the things that were said to you during your grief journey that were hurtful. (I have quoted verbatim throughout the book.)

- 🌳 Tell me the things that were said to you that were helpful. (I have paraphrased these suggestions.)

In addition to answering these questions, many voluntarily shared their experiences and described the circumstances around the death of their loved one. These stories included prolonged illnesses, brief terminal illnesses, suicides, accidental deaths and sudden natural deaths. I believe these details can assist us in understanding their reactions concerning those 'comforting' statements spoken by *well-intentioned* people. I have included, with permission, some of these stories in this book.

Despite the uniqueness of each grief journey, the respondents reported that people just did not know what to say to them and in their confusion they blurted out something that was hurtful.

In an effort to bring clarity to the subject of grief and mourning, I trust this book will help you to:

- hear the voices of grieving people in order for you to understand their journey;

- understand how to comfort grieving people when you don't know what to say;

- know how to respond when you experience *well-intentioned* people trying and failing to comfort you.

Please note that the lists throughout this book represent a sampling only of hundreds of responses.

Your life, exactly as it is,
contains just what is needed for your journey
of healing through the dark emotions.
It starts with learning to listen to your heart.

Miriam Greenspan

Chapter One: Setting the Stage

Defining the Terms: Clarifying Our Language

In every field of research, certain terms are used consistently. Important terms need to be defined and clarified so that we understand how the term is being used. For the purposes of this book, I have chosen definitions suggested by three notable researchers and authors in the field of grief and bereavement: Dr. K. Doka, Dr. W. Hoy, and Dr. A. D. Wolfelt (See Books and Articles Worth Noting at the end).

Below are definitions of the terms used throughout this book.

Bereavement means to be torn apart; to have special needs; to be robbed of someone.

Courage originates from the old French word for heart; helps us to open our hearts to receive care and comfort in our losses.

Dosing grief is grief we experience in small doses or waves, because we cannot embrace the pain of grief all at once. This allows grief to retreat until we are ready for the next wave.

Disenfranchised grief is grief that is not openly acknowledged, socially validated, or publicly observed; happens when a loss falls outside the 'norms' or 'parameters' established by a society, culture, faith culture, family or individual.

Emotion means 'energy in motion'; in order to be healthy, emotions must work for instead of against us. This requires befriending them.

Feeling comes from the Indo-European root word that means to touch. To feel is to activate your capacity to be touched and changed by experiences you encounter in life.

Grief is a collection of internal thoughts and feelings we have when someone we love dies; is the container that holds all of our thoughts, feelings, and images we experience when we are bereaved; is the internal meaning given to the experience of loss; is a natural and necessary response to the losses we encounter in our life journeys. *Carried grief* is grief unacknowledged and unmourned.

Healing in grief is to heal and become whole again; to integrate grief and to learn to continue living with fullness and meaning; is holistic and embraces the physical, emotional, cognitive, social and spiritual realms.

Mourning is the outward expression of grief and commonly referred to as 'grief gone public'.

Perinatal Death is a period of time "occurring or pertaining to the phase surrounding the time of birth, specifically the twentieth week of gestation to one to four weeks after birth" (The Oxford Dictionary).

Reconciliation occurs when one learns to consciously incorporate grief and proceed with meaning and purpose; is achieved when we have a renewed sense of energy and confidence; is an ability to acknowledge the full reality of the death and the capacity to become re-involved with the activities of living.

Suicide Survivor is a term that refers to those left behind; is not limited to family or close friends but any person who, in varying degrees; is in relationship with a person who has chosen to end their lives.

Unless you believe you are worthy of reconciliation and healing your suicide grief, you will question it, inhibit it, deny it, or push it away.

Alan D. Wolfelt

A wound that goes unacknowledged and unwept is a wound that cannot heal.

John Eldre

Whatever Became of the Stages of Grief?

A new way of understanding grief was ushered in with ground-breaking research and a book entitled, *On Death and Dying*, by psychiatrist Elizabeth Kubler-Ross in 1969. For many, this book offered a model for grief that was linear, clearly definable and eventually came to an end. To this day, it continues to be used by professionals as well as people who are grieving. In fact, this model has been so popular that it has even been applied in a broader context to other life situations such as experiencing a divorce, transitioning from one job to another, changing living accommodations and losing personal items, to name a few.

To understand this model's appeal, we need to understand the context. *On Death and Dying* came at a time when dying at home had been replaced with a hospital setting. This shift, from home to institutional care, had profound implications for both the dying and their families such as, families and friends often had limited access to their dying loved ones given the imposed restrictions by health care professionals and institutional policies.

As institutional care became entrenched in Western culture and with the population focused on conversations about death and in particular with the assassinations of President Kennedy and civil rights activist Martin Luther King Jr. plus the losses in the Vietnam War, people were ready for a linear, time sensitive model of death. As a result, a generation began to define a successful grief journey with how people manoeuvre effectively through the grief stages. Words like 'closure,' 'moving forward' and 'moving on' became part of the cultural vernacular and standard language of bereavement. (Interestingly, some years later, Kubler-Ross expressed dismay that she had introduced the word 'stages' as she never intended that this model be interpreted as a linear process (Doka, 2017, Online Webinar, *Living with Life Threatening Illness*).

Through the years, as research into grief and bereavement progressed, fresh insights immerged and new words to describe the experience were introduced. For instance, J. W. Worden (2009) began to use 'task' as a way to place greater emphasis on what one does to work through the grief process instead of the former understanding of how a grieving individual fits passively into a process. Furthermore, Worden outlined four distinct tasks that grieving people must grapple with: first, accept the reality of the loss; second, work through the pain of grief; third, adjust to an environment in which the deceased is missing; fourth, find an enduring connection with the deceased while embarking on a new life.

Influenced by Worden's work, Dr. Hoy (2014) envisioned a compass model to illustrate the grief journey, which considers the bereavement as a fluid process. Yet, to this day and despite all the challenges posed around understanding grief, all acknowledge that the best teachers are those who are experiencing or have experienced grief.

A New Model

Dr. B. Hoy (Used by Permission)

Hoy's new model identifies the unique needs of people who are grieving and rather than understanding grief as a 'stage' process, which seems to *clinicalize* the grief process, it focuses on the needs of all humans and the fluidity of the grief process that requires constant change and adaptation. For example, adaptation is necessary for: the widow whose husband handled the finances and after his death, she is now faced with signing cheques; or the young mother who cannot find the strength to dismantle the nursery after the death of her infant.

Compass Model of Bereavement: Finding Direction in Grief

Renewal is not a stage to 'go through' or a goal to be reached but rather the integration of grief into the life of the bereaved person in such a way that one learns to live a purposeful life while adapting to life without the loved one. Although grief never ends, Hoy suggests that, "the dysfunction of grief typically does". Unlike the prevailing linear stages model, grief is NOT something a person 'gets over' or 'finds closure'. Rather through story, memories and many other ways of embracing grief, one finds healthy ways to adapt.

Remembering helps grieving people to identify and embrace the stories and memories that have impacted them and their relationship to the deceased loved one. As the community joins in retelling the stories, the mourner needs to be encouraged to tell and retell their stories as often as necessary. All this affirms not only the life of the individual but the relationships that were vital to both the mourner and the one mourned.

Realizing helps mourners grapple with death and all its repercussions. However, Western culture is extremely reluctant to discuss this (Hoy, 2015) and therefore has a tendency to couch the language about death in phrases such as: passed on, no longer with us, passed away. Nonetheless, people, in an effort to acknowledge that death is real and that loss is forever life-changing, engage in various and diverse customs and rituals, such as funerals, memorial services and other such commemorations. These customs, regardless of the traditions, help "provide an invaluable foundation for healing to begin" (Hoy, 2015).

Releasing the loved one is a necessary but not a 'once and for all' accomplishment. Hoy (2015) suggests that, "We spend the rest of our lives saying goodbye" while moving ahead into new situations, new challenges and maybe even new living accommodations without the loved one. In other words, releasing, as part of the process of bereavement, is "really about finding new, rich ways to live life fully, even with the absence of our loved ones" (Hoy, 2015).

Reaffirming occurs when core values immerge and are examined. This often happens in the light of spirituality. Hoy suggests, "For many people, religious faith provides the cornerstone for this reaffirmation … through worship, prayer, or scripture reading" and regardless of whether bereaved people have a "conventional set of religious beliefs does not preclude them from finding spiritual meaning..."

The Power of Storytelling

Throughout the course of history, stories have been used in every culture and community to teach community values, connect to the past and to convey understanding, empathy and compassion. Despite the many formulas, theories, statistics and linear thinking we experience and most of which we've forgotten, stories remain a constant in our lives as the values and truths wrapped in a story connect us to one another.

For grieving people, storytelling remains an invaluable way of sharing their grief, making sense of their loss, reconciling their new reality with their grief, facing new challenges and finding the path forward. Even their deepest concerns and feelings make their way through their stories.

Also, stories are used to honour the deceased and through story the memory of their loved one is kept alive. Through story-sharing, listeners have an opportunity to ask open-ended questions and through this sharing, people can enter the lives of those grieving.

Stories can provide personal details of the deceased loved one otherwise not known to the family and friends. These stories often reflect the character traits of the individual such as honesty, humour and generosity. Regardless of whether the family was aware of these traits or not, they may not have been aware of the vast scope of influence their loved one had. These stories then, told by other family members, colleagues and friends contribute to the mosaic of the individual's life.

Storytelling not only reflects on the past, but provides opportunities to look to the future and the importance of legacy. Through storytelling, values are clarified and passed on to the next generation, who then are given the opportunity to embrace these positive values modeled by their departed family member.

Given the powerful importance of storytelling, those grieving need to be encouraged to tell their stories, when and where appropriate, regardless of how repetitive they may seem because this is an integral part of the grief process

Chapter Two: Adult Loss

Death of a Spouse

Facing the future together is often a dream that couples hold as they plan their lives together. These dreams may include raising a family, celebrating milestones and facing the ups and downs of life - together. For many, their plans may even extend to spending their senior years together.

However, when death occurs these dreams are shattered and with them all thoughts of 'togetherness'. The optimism and hope for the future is gone. For the one remaining, grief is profoundly deep and the notion of facing one more moment alone is overwhelmingly devastating while leaving in its wake a shattered heart and in its place the once bright future becomes a bleak future and an enemy of the soul.

In A Grief Observed, C. S. Lewis provides profound insights into his grief journey after the death of his beloved wife, Joy. He writes:

"No one ever told me that grief felt so like fear. I am not afraid, but the sensation is like being afraid. The same fluttering in the stomach, the same restlessness, the yawning. I keep on swallowing. At other times it feels like being mildly drunk, or concussed. There is a sort of invisible blanket between the world and me. I find it hard to take in what anyone says. Or perhaps, hard to want to take it in. It is so uninteresting. Yet I want the others to be about me. I dread the moments

when the house is empty. If only they would talk to one another and not to me."

The Power of Storytelling: Keith tells a widow's story

As I picked up the phone, there was a moment of silence at the other end and then I heard a voice that I recognized. Her words were abrupt, strong and angry. I recalled that she and her husband had just celebrated their 42nd wedding anniversary. How could they know within days of that wonderful celebration she would be making funeral arrangements?

Over the years he had kept himself in good physical shape and his yearly medical check-up had confirmed all was well. But one morning and without warning, he began gasping for air and he was gone.

Several months later, she called me to ask if I knew how to start a lawnmower. She said that this had always been 'his' job and that he had taken pride keeping the yard immaculate. Since the funeral, however, she had been watching the grass grow longer and longer but she couldn't bring herself to do anything about it nor ask anyone for help. But now, for whatever reason, she felt it was time to honour his memory by mowing the front lawn and despite her reluctance, she reached out for assistance. Later, she called again and through her tears reported her accomplishment and relief that she had taken this first gigantic step.

To me, mowing the lawn was not really the main

challenge for her but rather what the lawnmower represented ... she had been faced with her loss and the reality that she would never look out the front window again and see her beloved husband cutting the grass.

The Power of Storytelling: A Young Wife Remembers

As I opened the mailbox, I spotted a white envelope. I knew that it contained a cheque from the insurance company and though I had anticipated its arrival I could not bring myself to it. Early in our marriage, my husband and I had a decided to devise a plan in case one of us died so that the remaining one would be financially secure; but that was 'long term planning,' or so we thought. And now, three years later, my husband was dead and I was left alone to raise our young family.

So when the cheque arrived, I decided to put it in a desk drawer for a while. I knew the amount and had a good idea where the money would be spent, but that envelope represented the death of my beloved husband. My closest friends tried to help me by asking if I would be alright financially and they were relieved to know that the insurance money would provide stability. They even applauded me for the foresight we had in having a contingency plan in place. Some even said that I was 'lucky' not to have to worry about money. Others encouraged me to take time to enjoy life given all I'd been through, while others said I needed to go on a cruise. To reinforce their suggestions, they even said, "Your husband would have wanted you to do this!"

Tragically, no one acknowledged the reason why I had received the cheque in the first place. No one asked me how I felt about receiving the cheque. In an attempt to comfort me, my well-intentioned friends tried to present some positives. My heart was breaking and they were talking about 'fun' and 'luck'!

Hurtful words said to **grieving widowers** by *well-intentioned people*:

- x "She was such a wonderful person. Do you think you will re-marry?"
- x "She would not want you to be lonely."
- x "We have someone we would like you to meet."
- x "You are not going to stay in that house alone, are you?"
- x "Let me know when you are going to sell the house. I might have someone who is interested."
- x "It sure is going to be hard learning to do all the things she did."
- x "Thankfully her death was quick."
- x "You folks had a long life together. That has to be comforting."

- ✗ "Are you going to sell her car and if so, when and how much?"
- ✗ "Have you cried?"
- ✗ "Well, we all have to go sometime."
- ✗ "She lived a long life."
- ✗ "When do you think you will get over it?"
- ✗ "She is in a much better place now."

Hurtful words said to **grieving widows** by *well-intentioned* people:

- ✗ "Other wives told me that I was really lucky to be on my own, because now I could do whatever I wanted to do.
- ✗ "Keep busy; it will help."
- ✗ "He is in a better place."
- ✗ "At least it was quick. He would not have suffered."
- ✗ "I know how you must feel."
- ✗ "You're young. You will marry again. (Widowed at 23 years of age)
- ✗ "At least he is not suffering anymore."
- ✗ "You were such a great caregiver for such a long time. Didn't you feel relieved when he passed?
- ✗ "He finally won over the disease."

Hurtful words continued

x "I hope you will consider re-marrying quickly. It would be good for the children, given how young they are."

x "Your children are really young. In a way, this is a blessing that their dad died while they are young. Their loss will be easier."

x "Did he have a good life insurance policy? How do you think you will spend the money?"

x "You might want to give some thought to selling the house. You don't need such a large place anymore." (Advice given two months following funeral)

x "At least you have children to comfort you."

x "What a blessing that you were married for so many years."

x "He lived well beyond the expected years."

x "The last several years have not been good ones, have they?"

x "It was his time to go."

x "We were surprised he lasted so long given this was not his first heart attack."

× "How do you think you will spend the insurance money?"

× "I think a cruise is just what you need to take your mind off your loss." (Said three weeks following funeral)

× "When you get around to selling your house, will you let me know before you list? A good friend of mine might be interested." (Three months following funeral)

× "Regardless of age, I know many women who have found someone else, even if it is simply for companionship."

× "Would you seriously think of moving in with someone if you found someone 'special'?"

× "Do you plan on remarrying? (Said to grieving widow as she stood by her husband's casket.)

× "You look so much happier and relieved since he died."

Helpful words to say to **grieving spouses**:

- ✓ I would like to help but don't know what to do. Can you give me some ideas?
- ✓ Are there any practical things I can do like bring in bring in food or clean?
- ✓ You must miss her/him terribly.
- ✓ Any project you need help with?
- ✓ I am so sorry.
- ✓ You may not totally get over your loss, but you will learn to live with it.
- ✓ I am here if you need to talk.
- ✓ Don't let anyone tell you how to grieve. This is YOUR journey, not theirs.
- ✓ You do not have to be strong because you are a woman/man.
- ✓ It is OK if you want to return to work soon.
- ✓ You work out your grief the way you need to.
- ✓ Let me know, when you are ready, if you need help with her/his things.
- ✓ If you feel you want to talk to someone, I know a great counsellor to speak with.
- ✓ You were a great caregiver.

✓ She/he would have been proud of the way you are working with the kids.

✓ If you feel you want to go to a support group; I will go with you if you like.

Healers are hosts who patiently and carefully listen to the story of the suffering strangers.

Rabbi David Wolpe

Every time we make the decision to love someone, we open ourselves to great suffering, because those we most love cause us not only great joy, but also great pain. The greatest pain comes from leaving…the pain of the leaving can tear us apart. Still, if we want to avoid the suffering of leaving, we will never experience the joy of loving. And love is stronger than fear, life stronger than death, hope stronger than despair. We have to trust that the risk of loving is always worth taking.

Henry J. Nouwen

Death of a Parent – Grieving Adult Children

Most of us, as young children and then as adults, may unknowingly feel that our parents will always be with us. Somehow, death doesn't factor into our day-to-day thinking even when we know our parents are aging or perhaps even ailing. When faced with the death of a parent, the age or circumstance doesn't matter; the grief experienced is nonetheless deep and profound.

Parents are a link to the past, for many adult children. They are the ones who held and retold the stories of previous generations and recalled stories of their children's childhood - stories such as first steps, first tooth, first day at school or first mishap. They may have also represented stability, security and love. While their children were finding their place in the world and all that entails, parents could be relied on to provide stability and support. Consequently, the death of a parent can invoke strong memories and feelings that perhaps spans decades.

Through the years, parents may have also represented wisdom and experience. In healthy relationships, adult children may have instinctively looked to their parents for guidance, support and encouragement. Conversely, some may have experienced tumultuous childhoods and then the death of a parent can bring memories that had been forgotten or buried for years. As a result, grief can be compounded by bittersweet or embittered memories.

Regardless of the circumstances, age or nature of the relationship, grieving adult children will embark on a journey of revisiting their childhood, their relationship with their parent and relationship with their family of origin.

The Power of Storytelling: A Son Remembers

We had anticipated dad's death for quite some time; after all, he was ninety-one. Numerous doctors' appointments and multiple hospital admissions had prepared us for his final hospital stay - or so we thought. This last hospital stay lasted twenty-one days, with several 'close calls'. Over the course of these days, dad was lucid to the point that we were lulled into believing he might even come home ... one more time.

It is hard to distinguish between our hopes, desires and reality. Our minds understood he was slowly leaving us but our hearts kept hoping that perhaps we would have more time with him. Each day, we became more emotionally torn as we watched and waited.

Funny, the things you think and talk about as family over the course of the days spent waiting in a small, quiet, private hospital room. Usually, the conversations began with storytelling and often began with, "Do you remember when?" Dad would participate in the conversations when he could.

Even in the silent moments, we reflected with thanksgiving and tears. The 'family baton' was being

---

passed to the next generation. Our strong, decisive, father was slowly losing strength and control.

We promised dad that a family member would be present when he passed and that promise seemed to give him a sense of peace and calm. We knew the ever-increasing pain medication would place him in a deep sleep.

Late one night the call came. Although we knew it was coming, we were still surprised when we heard the nurse's voice saying, "You need to come now, your dad is close."

Dad died soon after we all arrived. We had time to say our good-byes and then he was gone. The hospital staff told us that there was no rush to leave afterwards. This in itself was comforting to know.

My story ends with a brief observation. During the time of visitation, funeral and the gathering afterword, very few people acknowledged our pain and sorrow. Wonderful tributes were given to our father but for the most part, his age seemed to be the focus of their comments. I know well-intentioned *people did not mean to dismiss our grief but in our hearts, this is exactly how it felt when they said, " He was ninety-one. I am sure you are thankful you had him for so many years. He lived a long life." We were well aware of his age and we were grateful for the years he was with us, but grief and mourning are things experienced in the heart. Actually, it was the longevity of his life that made saying good-bye so difficult and challenging.*

Hurtful words said by *well-intentioned* people to **grieving adult children**:

- x "Well, he lived such a long life. You should be grateful."
- x "Why all the tears? After all, given his age and deteriorating health; this was not a surprise."
- x "He is probably happy now that he's with your mother."
- x "How old was he anyway?"
- x "He lived longer than most people."
- x "God must have needed her."
- x "She's in a better place."
- x "She wouldn't want you to be sad."

Helpful words to say to **grieving adult children**:

- ✓ I imagine you have wonderful memories of him.
- ✓ The way you honoured him at his funeral was perfect and the family involvement was key. He would have loved that.
- ✓ Your mom/dad loved you very much and was so proud of you.
- ✓ I can't imagine how you feel right now but know I'm here for you.

Chapter Three: Death of a Baby Child – Teen

Imagine the news … "You're pregnant!" and all the accompanying feelings evoked in knowing that a new life will be coming to your family: excitement, trepidation, anticipation like no other. Your lives will be changed forever. From the very beginning, you start to dream of your future with this little person and envision what he will look like, what sort of personality she will have.

This anticipation and future-vision continues throughout pregnancy, childbirth, toddlerhood, childhood and even into the teen years. Questions like "Will she have her father's fiery red hair?" morph into "Will these two-year-old tantrums be indicative of his adult personality?" and finally into "What sort of adult will my spirited teen turn out to be and how will he contribute to his society?" Though parents will experience a range of thoughts and emotions during various seasons of life, a common thread throughout the parenting journey is that of hope for the future with their child and a sense of family legacy that will be embodied by the life of the child.

But now imagine the news… "Your baby has died!" or "There has been an accident!" or "Your child has a terminal illness." Despite the age or surrounding circumstances, the death of your child is unlike any other loss. The world as you once knew now no longer exists. You immediately experience a double-whammy of grief: the proper order of life has been turned on its head (a parent should never have to bury their child) and the dreams of your child's future have been irrevocably shattered. As news of your child's death settles into your new life reality, your identity becomes redefined; your role as provider, protector and guide has dissolved and you begin to search for answers to questions about purpose, meaningfulness, spirituality, life and death and ultimately: **"Why, Why, Why?"**

Though child loss is a category of grief all on its own, some unique themes specific to the age of the child can be identified. In examining the stories of those who have lost children, I have discovered that they fall into three distinct categories and I will unpack each separately as follows:

- Perinatal loss – miscarriage and stillbirth
- Child loss – toddlers and pre-teens
- Teen loss

Perinatal loss

Perinatal loss is the term used to describe the death of a fetus during pregnancy through miscarriage, abortion, stillbirth (death occurs at the end of the pregnancy) or neonatal death (death occurs soon after delivery). Some have referred to perinatal grief as "the silent, unspoken loss".

This grief is as real, deep and life altering as any other kind of death loss but is often minimized due to the short duration of time that the relationship has had to develop. Usually those who have experienced other losses have memories of the person who died, but memories do not exist for those who have lost a fetus or baby. More disturbing is the fact that Western culture generally does not recognize miscarriage as a legitimate loss and therefore not worthy of an equal grieving process for parents. For example, the Province of Ontario does not recognize the death of a fetus if it occurs within the twenty weeks of gestation and such death then is not recorded with Vital Statistics. This lack of recognition has a tremendously negative impact on grieving parents because if a society generally does not recognize this loss, those grieving are typically not validated nor are they encouraged to conduct any type of ritual (funeral, memorial service) that might be typically held after any other loss.

Furthermore, other unique aspects to the grief associated with miscarriage, stillbirth and neonatal death is the unanticipated reminders of the life gone and a future that can no longer be anticipated. For instance, during pregnancy mothers are bombarded with baby-associated product discounts, links to websites with parenting information, community baby services, etc. However, long after the baby's death, emails and pamphlets will continue to arrive and people continue to ask about the expected due date, which only serves as a constant reminders of the loss.

The Power of Storytelling: A Parent Remembers

From the moment the doctor confirmed our suspicions, we went into 'parent mode' and began to put a plan together, which included the decision to wait for a few months before telling anyone our news. This plan began with the conversion of the spare room into a nursery We thought that nine months would go by fast and it did!

We don't remember many of the details about the news we received later from the doctor, but we will never forget … "I'm so sorry; it just happens."

As we sat in the visitation room with our family and a few chosen friends, we couldn't take our eyes off the small, white casket. So many questions raced through our minds: Why did the minister say it was God who chose to take our daughter? Why did he tell them God never gives you more than you can handle? Why did my well-intentioned *mother whisper in my ear we were leaving the room, "Just be thankful the doctor told you another baby is possible; just give it some time"?*

However long the night, the dawn will break.

An African Proverb

The Power of Storytelling: A Mother's Story

Over the years and in varying circumstances, I've often heard people say, "At times there are just no words to describe how you feel inside," and as I recall there have been several times when words have failed me. But when our baby died, we experienced a pain and sorrow that was unfathomably deep.

I had suspected I was pregnant for several weeks prior to the doctor's appointment. I hadn't said anything to my husband because I knew he would morph immediately into 'Tim the Tool Man' mode and want to renovate the entire house. But finally, I told him and made the doctor's appointment to confirm my suspicion. We were ecstatic! This would be our first baby!

We talked about the first time we would hold our baby. Would he or she have hair and if so, what colour? Would the baby be small or huge? Would the baby cry upon arrival or simply be quiet with little movement? What would it feel like to have the baby placed on my chest for the first time? Of course, my husband couldn't resist talking about the tools he would need to buy in order to build the nursery. He assured me it would be the nursery of the century.

Together we dreamed and our dreams had no boundaries. We talked about the first day of kindergarten and walking hand in hand - all three of us, to that big building down the street and saying good-bye. I even found myself crying at the thought of leaving our first-born. We fantasied about every aspect of our child's life. We even pre-planned a trip to Disneyland and then moved on to talk about the rules for boys dating our teen age daughter.

These conversations would remain in our hearts forever. They would become both a source of strength and sorrow for none of it became a reality. The fact is, our reality changed in a moment. All I remember clearly is that late fall night and the words of the doctor in the delivery room, "I am so sorry. It does not happen often." I will spare you the details but needless to say, we moved from our fantasy world of dreams and hopes to making funeral arrangements.

The small, intimate funeral was by invitation only; this was a time for our immediate families and a few close friends to gather. There are no words to describe that night as we walked into the candlelit room and saw the small white casket at the front surrounded by floral arrangements.

I really don't remember many things the pastor said but one thing riveted deeply into my heart. Sometime during the service, he gave my husband and I a single puzzle piece. As he handed it to us he said, "Your grief is like this puzzle. It is going to come to you one piece at a time. Every month I am going to send you a piece in the mail. Each piece will not make any sense at the time. However, keep them. Eventually you will have the entire picture, the whole puzzle, the whole picture."

Well, it has been over three years from that day and he was right. Our grief was day to day. Some days we hardly felt like getting out of bed; other days were less painful as our lives had been changed forever. There are still many moments when we wonder, question and think 'what if' but those times are becoming less and less.

When we received the last piece of the puzzle, we put the puzzle together and placed it behind a glass frame where it now hangs in our family room where our two-year-old son always points to the beautiful mountain scene.

Hurtful words said to **grieving parents** by *well-intentioned* people:

- × "At least there was not much time to become attached".
- × "It is a blessing you did not proceed to make any more plans".
- × "Did you begin putting a nursery together".
- × "You did not name the baby so early, did you?"
- × "Thank God you have another child".
- × "It probably would have been abnormal anyway".
- × "Nature has a way of balancing things out, doesn't it?"
- × "This was for the best; someday you will recognize it".

Hurtful words continued

x "You are lucky you survived".

x "Now that it is over, you can get on with your life and make plans".

x "It's a good thing you did not spend a lot of money getting ready".

x "Is there anyone you can think of who can use your maternity clothes or maybe a place you can drop off the clothes".

x "Better luck next time".

x "Are you going to try again?"

x "Remember, lightning doesn't strike twice".

x "Time will help you heal".

x "God only took your baby because of His great love for children".

x "Perhaps God is trying to teach you something".

x "God never gives us more than we can handle; that's what the Bible says".

x "Is there anything you can think of that made God mad or displeased with you?"

x "Keep meditating on all the promises in the Bible. This will get you through".

- x "The Bible says all testing has a Divine purpose".
- x "This can be a witness to those who do not believe".
- x "My mother used to tell me…when bad things happen to you, look for someone worse off; it will help"'
- x "Now you have an angel in Heaven looking down on you".
- x "Maybe your faith was not strong enough to overcome this one".
- x "At least it was not human yet."
- x "Someday you will see your baby in Heaven".

Helpful words to comfort after a **perinatal loss**:

- ✓ I am so sorry.
- ✓ I cannot imagine what you must be feeling.
- ✓ Is there anything I can possibly do for you?
- ✓ I don't know what to say, or what to do.
- ✓ Tell me - What is your baby's name?
- ✓ I hope you are going to have a funeral, even if it is by invitation only.

- ✓ If you'd like to - Can you tell me what happened?
- ✓ What is your doctor saying to you?
- ✓ Where is your baby buried?
- ✓ Did you pick a name? What was the name and was there significance to the name?
- ✓ Tell me about the funeral.

Too often, we underestimate the power of a touch, a smile, a kind word, a listening ear, an honest compliment, or the smallest act of caring, all of which have the potential of turning a life around.

Leo Buscaglia

Child Loss

With the loss of a child the 'right and proper order of life' is destroyed and with this destruction the dreams for the next generation are dashed. Life, as the parents once knew it, has been replaced with the horrific pain of having lost a part of themselves; an amputation has occurred and life must be faced without their beloved child.

Author Judith Bernstein penned these words in *When the Bough Breaks*:

> *We know our grief will never end; we will never return to our old selves. But one day we will be able to enjoy the bittersweet strains of a melody; laughter is not out of the question. We will live again, transformed in every aspect of our lives.*

For every parent, a child represents a myriad of thoughts, feelings and fears. Yet, one thought seems to be constant: a child represents not only a link to the past but also to the future. The past and all that it means to the family is embodied in the birth and story of a child while dreams of this child embraces a future with all its hope and promise.

The Power of Storytelling: A Mother's Story

Our daughter was only four years of age. From all outward appearances, she seemed well; a normal little girl but little did we know while we were enjoying our wonderfully energetic daughter, a tiny, undetected enemy of the heart was lurking just beneath the surface.

Her symptoms, at first, were relatively 'normal' and therefore we treated them accordingly as. We were so pleased how quickly our physician acted to refer us to a specialist.

Then, without warning, this enemy attacked. This very rare heart disease compromised her heart and a few days later, she died. I will never forget the specialist's words when he said, "We have no explanation other than to say this condition is so rare that it goes undetected until it is virtually too late." With those devastating words, the future became unbelievably dark and scary.

I remember one of the many challenges of grieving was people's insistence that we give a detailed explanation as to how, in this day and age, such a thing could happen. Their constant insistence felt more like probing than inquiring. In fact, we often had to find reasons to end the conversation in order to escape the barrage.

In other instances, people just didn't know what to say to us so they avoided contacting us or conversations became very awkward and superficial. There were even times when I felt I could hear them say, under their breath, "I am so sorry for your loss but so glad it didn't happen to us."

We have discovered that time, in and of itself, does not heal anything. However, as we learn to take one day at a time and sometimes moment-by-moment, we are gradually learning to embrace and celebrate the four short years we had with her. When the anniversary of her birthday arrives or when we watch her friends playing, we find ourselves wondering what she would have been like now, if she had lived.

Oh, be the way, we didn't move away from our neighborhood, as some advised us to do. Some people thought our house and neighborhood held too many painful memories. Yet, we have discovered that our memories bring us great solace and comfort.

Be not afraid, of going slowly, be afraid of only standing still.

Chinese Proverb

Hurtful words said to **grieving parents** by *well-intentioned* people:

×   "Well there is no sense being upset." (sitting in front of son's casket)

×   "Don't let him go. We will love him anyway." (removal of life support decision)

×   "Just pretend he is a dog; it isn't so hard that way."

×   "Things die; it happens."

×   "Don't worry; you will have another baby - lots of babies."

×   "Do you want us to pack up everything for you, including all clothes, toys and nursery when you get home it will all be gone that will help." (offer was made when mother took two days away before returning to her house)

×   "Why are you so depressed? I thought you said you were doing ok."

×   "You are crazy and you are driving all of us nuts. Get some therapy."

×   "You will see him again."

×   "He is in a better place."

× "It was for the best; he would have suffered too much."

× "I think he chose to leave this life because of the situation in your home and go to a different home, a better and much calmer one."

× "You must be a terrible mother to let him die."

× "Please do not tell my any more. I don't want to think about it anymore. It makes me too sad."

× "Just try to forget." … "Time heals all wounds."

× "Keep busy."

× "Go do something you enjoy."

× "Just have another baby quickly."

× "It's been a year … why are you still so upset?"

× "You have another child now doesn't that make up for the one lost?"

× "Are you always going to miss him?"

× "You have to be happy for your other child now."

× "You are going to upset your child by crying at Christmas and other holidays."

× "Let go - move on." "Start living again."

× "Everything happens for a reason."

Helpful words to say to **grieving parents** after the **loss of a child**:

- ✓ He/she was a beautiful baby.
- ✓ This is not fair, this is not your fault.
- ✓ You are a great mom; he misses you.
- ✓ You will miss him so much.
- ✓ We will never forget him.
- ✓ Tell me what happened. Only tell me what you want to tell. Leave any details out you wish.
- ✓ I can hold some of your pain for you until you feel you are able to feel it.
- ✓ Tell me about all your pain; let me carry it with you.
- ✓ Please feel free to share the horrible details around the death and circumstances. I will hold whatever you say in the strictest of confidence.
- ✓ Feel free to share your feelings with me.
- ✓ If you want, I would like to see a picture of your son/daughter.
- ✓ How are your thoughts doing today?
- ✓ Can I share some happy memories I have of your son/daughter with you?
- ✓ Teach me how I can help.

- ✓ I was thinking about your son/daughter today.
- ✓ Can I come to the cemetery with you, when you are ready?
- ✓ Please take care of yourself.
- ✓ You did the most unselfish thing a person could do by letting go. (making the decision to remove life-support)
- ✓ I got a cute gift today for your son. Can you take it to the cemetery?
- ✓ Let me know if there's anything I can do for you.
- ✓ When you're ready to talk, I will listen without judging or criticising you.

Our lives have become changed, but without our permission.

Elizabeth H. Neeld

Teen Loss

No one, least of all parents, is ever prepared for the death of their teen. For most parents, the thought that their son or daughter will not live beyond their teens is unimaginable. Through the teen years and while their teens continue to become more autonomous, parents instinctually continue to want to protect. So when death occurs, it shatters this natural instinct to protect and the reality hits as a stark reminder that despite all their best efforts, no one can be completely protected. This utter feeling of helplessness will daunt parents afterwards and will often continue for years later.

The Power of Storytelling: A Dad's Story

Like many fathers, I dreamed about the day I would climb into the family car with my teenage son at the wheel for the first time. When that dream became a reality for me, it almost felt like a right of passage for both my son and I.

On that important 'first' day, I couldn't help but take a moment and think back to my son's birth and all the times we had shared up to this point. Where did all the years go? And now I'm taking my son out for his first driving lesson!

After going through the rudiments of driving, I could tell he was anxious to put the car in drive and go. Every lesson I would give from this moment until he was ready to drive on his own was couched in the same truth, "Driving is a huge responsibility son and safety and speed are your responsibilities."

It wasn't too long before he had completed his instruction and received his license and then he was off to explore the world without his dad sitting in the passenger seat giving instructions.

One Friday, I had returned home from a long week at work and he asked if he could use the car to go into town to meet up with some friends. The plan was simple; he would pick up his long-time best friend who lived a few houses away and they would make the short trip to town, together. Once we established a curfew, I tossed him the keys and he was off. As I recall, the weather and the road conditions were fine that night.

After supper, I settled in for an evening of watching television, knowing full well, I would be dozing in and out in my comfortable chair. After a few short hours, the doorbell rang. My wife was out at the time and so I made my way to the door. To my surprise, when I opened the door I was greeted by a police officer and another man, who was not in uniform. The officer asked for my name and asked if they could come in. Their first words will haunt me for the rest of my life, "We are sorry to inform you there has been an accident. Your son and his passenger have been killed." I asked them to repeat what they had just said. I listened; then slumped to the floor. As it happened, my son had chosen to ignore the repeated lecture on speeding. Apparently, he decided to 'try out' the speed of the car and he lost control, hit the pebbled shoulder of the road and was propelled over a ditch into an open field where they collided into a large tree. Death had come in a moment.

That first weekend and the following weeks are a blur. I vaguely recall making our way to the funeral home to make arrangements.

No one can ever be prepared for such a devastating event like this one. My stomach still turns when the doorbell rings. People, for the most part, were and continue to be gracious and kind but they still do not know what to say or how to say anything that will relieve the pain.

It has been several years now since that fateful night. In a way, it still feels surreal yet every time I walk by my son's room I am reminded, that this is not an awful dream! We talk about him everyday and through the tears thank God he was our son, even if is was for only a short period of time.

Hurtful words said to **grieving parents** by *well-intentioned* people:

- ✕ "In a way this must come as a relief. He was such a troubled teen."

- ✕ "Are you going to pursue legal action against the drug deal?"

- ✕ "If he hadn't stolen your car, this wouldn't have happened."

× "Thank God it happened quickly."

× "Your daughter should never have been running with that crowd."

× "Did you not see the signs of darkness around him? We did."

× "Save yourself and your family the embarrassment and have a private funeral."

× You are strong.

× If this happened to me, I would not survive.

× Don't your think you have too many pictures of your daughter on the wall?

× Why do you need a counsellor when you have family?

× Just think how many clothes you now get to wear. (said to sibling re: her deceased sister)

People say losing a child is the worst. I know of nothing more accurate. It's like joining a club you don't want to belong to and you're in it for life.

John Hewett

Helpful words to say to **grieving parents** on the death of their **teen**:

- ✓ I am so sorry for your loss.
- ✓ He/she was a special person.
- ✓ Take all the time you need to grieve.
- ✓ I can't imagine what you are going through and I am not going to try.
- ✓ You are not alone.
- ✓ There is support in the community for you when you think you are ready.
- ✓ Don't beat yourself up.
- ✓ Do you need a hug?
- ✓ Be kind to yourself.
- ✓ Remember, your journey is different than your husband's.
- ✓ Your son sure packed a lot of life in such a few short years.
- ✓ We always enjoyed him in our home.
- ✓ Our home will feel the absence of his presence
- ✓ You were great parents
- ✓ She was so respectful of you
- ✓ He always bragged about the great home he came from.

Chapter Four: Death by Suicide

The unthinkable has happened; a family member has committed suicide. No one suspected that this could ever be possible. There were no signs or clues that would lead the family or friends to believe this was going to happen. In shock, the family reels from their loss and the nature of the death. This death has impacted not only close family, but friends, colleagues and the broader community.

The family knows that people in the community are whispering as rumours and speculations begin to circulate. The family becomes the focus of attention as people whisper questions amongst themselves – "What was happening in the family to cause this person to do this?"; "Surely there were signs that the family missed?"; "How could anyone *not* know?"

Sadly, the family and even their friends are left alone to grapple with their own haunting questions, overwhelming grief and funeral arrangements all the while contending with the perceptions, speculations and misunderstandings of the larger community. As if their loss wasn't enough, they must now think about how to answer people's questions and how to respond to their show of concern.

Generally, every culture, family and faith community adheres to certain kinds of acceptable and normal grief patterns, practices and expressions of comfort. Death by suicide, by its very nature, is placed outside these boundaries of what is commonly accepted and viewed as normal. As a result, the death of a loved one by suicide throws families into a deep, dark and lonely abyss that causes untold devastation.

The Power of Storytelling: *Keith recalls a mother's story of a son's suicide*

"I simply have to tell my story," she told me (Keith). She explained that in the beginning she and her husband thought that they would never share what happened because of the shame, guilt, stigmatization and overwhelming pain they were experiencing.

This mom went on to say that not too long after our son's death, we thought we were alone and that there was no one we could talk to who would really know what it was like. Thankfully, we were wrong. People like us, who have experienced this kind of loss, began to approach us. We did not for a moment see them as intruders but rather friends.

There are no words to describe the horrible, gut-wrenching situation of finding our fourteen-year-old son, or the panicked call for help and then to watch the firefighters attempting to revive him but only to hear, "He is gone. I am so sorry."

Immediately, you go into shock, denial and then tremendous anger. Uncontrollable crying soon was replaced with numbness. I still can see and hear all the people who were filling our home. Their voices were distant and muffled. Family members soon arrived. I remember thinking, "Who called them? I didn't."

I am ashamed to admit this but my husband, older son and I always believed that this kind of thing only happened to 'certain' kinds of people, and 'certain' kinds of homes. I also believed that when someone took their life, there was always a reason and there must have certainly been hints along the way that the family had overlooked. I would look at such homes and secretly wonder what 'kind' of parents and what 'kind' of home did this young person come from where this sort of thing was even possible? I was so wrong!

I imagine what I am about to say will, for some, maybe misunderstood or even dismissed, yet these are the facts.

We were the family that did life together; we loved, laughed and cried together. As with all families, we had our challenges, but nothing we couldn't handle as a family. Our home was a safe place. We were a loving family and free to show our love for each other and indeed we would often joke that each of us was born with our emotions on our sleeves and would never need professional help to discover our true and buried feelings. At school, the kids were doing well and even beginning to show an interest in subjects that might point them towards future careers.

So why? That is always the question isn't it? Even if there was a note or signs along the way (and there wasn't), I have come to understand and accept that no one will ever really know the reason why a person looks at their life and cannot find a reason to continue living and then chooses not to.

Our family is still not prepared to say that death by suicide and all that follows is worse than any other loss. As someone once shared, "Loss is loss, pain is pain and love covers it all." However, there are some unique aspects to our journey, which make it really challenging to navigate and process. We will forever be 'the' family and our house 'the' home where their son died.

Several years have passed since that horrible day yet we still get glances from some and we still feel scrutinized by others. I imagine them saying to themselves, "So glad that was not us - not our son/daughter!"

As a family, we chose not to simply survive this tragic and life-altering event but instead we've chosen to learn how to live life fully, again. A fellow suicide survivor once said, "This loss is like losing an arm or leg. You know it is gone but you still feel a phantom pain as if it is still attached."

I certainly can't tell you all the ways we're coping and living with our loss. However, one central idea comes to mind. We have chosen to concentrate on the years we had with our dear son. We are not, by any means, in denial. He is gone and we mourn his passing every day. However, we keep telling our stories about him. That one moment changed us forever but it did not eradicate the years before when he was alive, fully engaged and fully a part of our family.

Do we cry as we tell our stories? Yes! Do we laugh? Yes! Are we profoundly thankful for our son, his life and his legacy? Oh, yes!

Hurtful words said to **grieving parents** by *well-intentioned* people:

- × "How did he die?"
- × "Which method of suicide did he chose?"
- × "Why would he choose that way over …?"
- × "Did he suffer from depression?"
- × "Did he leave a note and if so, what did he say?"
- × "Would a note, if had left one, been more comforting for your family?"
- × "How are you doing? How are you feeling?"
- × "Do you think suicide is something that runs in your family?"
- × "Is it possible your doctor missed something?"
- × "What did the coroner's report say?"
- × "Was she thinking about it for very long?"
- × "How did you find her?"
- × "What drove him to take his life?"
- × "Is it possible you missed the clues?"

Hurtful words … continued

- x "Does mental illness run in your family?"

- x "You will get over it in time."

- x "It's a good thing your children are still very young. Have you given any thought to what you will tell them later on about their father?"

- x "I am so sorry for your loss but I know the Bible says anyone who takes their life spends eternity in hell."

- x "You will find a new normal."

- x "When I saw him last, he seemed so happy. What do you think when wrong?"

- x "Do you think you will sell the house right away? How can you go in the house everyday knowing it took place there?

- x "My best friend's son took his life ten years ago. She has never been the same since."

- x "We all thought you guys had the perfect marriage, home and family. Any idea what went wrong?"

- x "We had no idea he was so unhappy."

- x "Come on. It's been three months now and it's time you get out. You'll feel better."

Helpful things to say **grieving parents** after the loss of a loved one to **suicide**:

- ✓ I understand if you want to be alone right now.

- ✓ When you want, I will come over with a box of tissue and we can cry together. I will call first to see if it is OK to visit.

- ✓ It is no one's fault.

- ✓ There is nothing you say or feel that will affect our friendship. Remember, we are in this together for the long haul.

- ✓ We have missed you at … but that is OK. When you are ready, let me know and I will sit with you.

- ✓ You don't have to try make us feel better.

- ✓ I know you feel like everyone is looking at you but they aren't. They just don't know what to say and they don't want to hurt you anymore than you are.

- ✓ It must really hurt you that no one can really know how you feel.

- ✓ I am not going to try to fix you but know this…I'm here.

- ✓ Please know I don't need to know any details.

Helpful things … continued

- ✓ You are a great mom. I know you do not think it right now but someday you will.
- ✓ I have recently read a few books on suicide and what you are experiencing is absolutely normal.

When the suicide bomb dropped….one group of people is always standing at ground zero, the members of the surviving family.

Barbara Roberts

Chapter Five: Returning to the Workplace

After receiving an invitation to present an hour-long seminar on the topic of how to handle employees returning to the workplace after a death loss, I was faced with a challenge. Aside from the logistics of the time restraint, I wondered if perhaps this invitation to conduct a brief seminar represented a cultural understanding or rather a misunderstanding regarding grief and the impact on the workplace. It seemed to me that I was being asked to, "Tell us what we need to know, in an hour, in order to deal with this problem."

Too often the focus on the company's business plans and goals can overshadow the good intentions of the employer who wants to be empathetic to an employee who is struggling with grief and the ensuing ramifications. For most, grief can include sporadic emotional waves, lack of concentration, overwhelming fatigue and may often leave the employer in a dilemma as to how to support the employee while ensuring that the work continues.

The Power of Storytelling: Grieving Employee Remembers Returning to Work

For years, I was the top salesman in my company and had received many accolades attesting to my skills that the president of the company asked me to train the junior sales people. For me, this was a dream come true. I loved the company, the product and the endless opportunities for advancement.

Then it happened; I lost the love of my life – my wonderful wife. My world shattered. I changed. Everything changed.

Because of my standing in the company, my boss informed me at the funeral, that I could take an additional week off to "clear my head and get everything in order". After that week off, I had to face the inevitable journey back to the office. That morning, as I stood in front of the mirror, buttoning my shirt and tying my tie I saw a stranger staring back at me whose hollow eyes and expressionless face I did not recognize. For this stranger, life seemed to have disappeared or at least been driven deeply into an abyss of sorrow and pain.

I arrived at work early. I knew walking into an empty office would not solve anything but I thought at least it would be a safe entry before the office filled up with staff who were eager to greet the day and sell. My boss arrived shortly after my arrival and summoned me into his large, ornately furnished office. After a brief greeting, he asked the question I had been dreading, "Do you think, given your current state of affairs, you

> *will be able to meet or exceed your monthly sales quota?"*

Hurtful words said by *well-intentioned* people to a returning, **grieving employee**:

× "Perhaps you should take the family pictures off your desk."

× "We have moved your desk to the corner so if you start crying, the rest of the office will not be able to see you."

× "If you must cry at work, would you please excuse yourself and go to the washroom."

× "Do you think there is any way you could not cry while at work?"

× "Is there any way you could wear more waterproof make-up so your crying is not so obvious to other?"

× "We have taken several client accounts away from you for a time until you can get it together like you were before."

× "We understand your grief but the focus for this business is sales, positive thinking and satisfaction."

Hurtful words … continued

× "I hate to ask, but do you have an idea as to when the worst part of your grief will be over and how long it will take before you are back to your 'old self'?"

× "Now that you're back, do you think you will be able to keep up with the work load?"

Helpful words to say to a **returning, grieving employee**:

✓ We have no idea what you are going through. Would you help us to understand how we can help?

✓ We don't understand what you are going through but if there are times at work you need to go and cry or need to leave, just do it. We are here for you.

✓ We will keep a good supply of Kleenex in your desk and in the stock room.

✓ Please keep the family pictures on your desk if it brings you comfort.

✓ Don't stop telling your stories about…. .

- ✓ If you need to take some extended lunch hours, do so.
- ✓ You let me know when you are ready to come back. We will hold down the fort until you do.
- ✓ Take a few weeks. Keep in touch with us to let us know how you are doing.
- ✓ Is it OK if the office staff takes care of meals for the next several weeks? Any favorite foods or dietary restrictions?

We bereaved are not alone. We belong to the largest company in all the world, the company of those who have known suffering.

Helen Keller

I've had the kind of day, no quote can fix.

R.E. Goodrich

Chapter Six: Where do we go from here?

In thinking about the many years I have spent listening to and walking with people on their grief journey, I am struck not only by their courage in the face of devastating loss but their willingness to help me and others understand their journey. They are extraordinary teachers. With their help, I have created the following summary that can help *you* if you experiencing grief or wanting to comfort someone who is grieving:

About Grief

- Grief and mourning are messy. There is no prescribed formula or time line.
- Grief needs an outlet and the expression of grief is called mourning.
- Grief cannot be 'fixed'; words will not alleviate the pain.
- Grief can provide a way for us to find new meaning and direction for our lives.
- Grief is hard work and taxes the physical, emotional, intellectual and spiritual resources of grieving people.

🌱 Grief is all-consuming, confusing, heartbreaking debilitating and often misunderstood by others.

🌱 Grief is always felt, no matter the circumstances of the death or age of the person who died.

🌱 Grief is expressed differently in every person.

🌱 Grief if not experienced will not be understood and any *well-intentioned* attempt to offer words of support often fall short or often become hurtful.

🌱 Grief can often be compounded by the *well-intentioned* comments that bring hurt.

About Grieving People

🌱 The first year after the loss is not harder just different; this year tends to be exceptionally busy with estate matters and many 'firsts'.

🌱 Mourners need to process their deep feelings with a safe person so that the grieving process does not turn into resentment.

🌱 People on their grief journey can find wholeness and find a new way of living life.

🌱 People need to process their grief in meaningful ways.

- People need to find a 'safe' person with whom to confide.
- For some, expressing their grief through tears is healthy and therapeutic.
- For some, finding healthy expressions of grief does not mean crying.
- People need to tell their story as part of the grief journey.
- Funerals are important but do not 'bring closure'.
- Funerals bring people together to mourn and celebrate a life.
- Rituals are crucial to healing.
- Beneficial eulogies provide a time for honesty, laughter and tears.
- Regardless of the age or situation, grief is grief and is felt no less because of the age of the person who has died.
- Storytelling is powerful: by telling stories, the loved one is honoured and the mosaic of the person's life becomes more complete.

Courage doesn't always roar. Sometimes courage is the little voice at the end of the day that says, "I'll try again tomorrow."

Mary Anne Radmacher

About Funerals, Rituals and Ceremonies

Not long ago, the words funeral and celebration were never spoken in the same sentence. Today, however, people are expressing grief in a myriad of creative ways. Over the years, I have learned what seems to be the most effective way to begin the grieving journey. For instance:

Funerals create space and a deliberate moment to permit us to reflect on the deeper things of life, its meaning and purpose. During this reflective time, we are encouraged to make necessary life changes as we acknowledge and embrace our core values. This time helps reinforce not only our values but also helps us to embrace and celebrate the values passed on by the deceased. Funerals can also act as a collective 'send off' much like the rituals we experience at the birth of a baby.

Rituals acknowledge the passage of life. They reaffirm and confront us again with the universality of death. They are a way of honouring the one who has died. For those left behind, rituals assist us in marking a loss, celebrating the life, allowing the healing process to begin.

Ceremonies help us to grapple with and reinforce the reality of our loss and assist us understand something about the nature of death. They help us draw near to our Creator and to one another.

Lament plays a crucial part in the grieving process. Words found in sacred scriptures, readings, poems, art work, mementos, all speak for us and to us.

Community plays an important role in grieving and mourning. Through community, funerals are performed as people gather to mourn and to support and comfort one another and those grieving.

Helpful ways to comfort grieving people

Be sensitive to cultural differences. Cultural traditions are important and need to be understood, respected and honoured. Therefore:

- Be aware of your own feelings: suspend giving advice and pronouncing judgement.
- Be careful your story of grief doesn't overshadow the one who is telling their story.
- Be trustworthy. Holding a confidence is vital and provides safety. Repeating someone else's story creates mistrust.
- Be honest – if you don't know what to say, say nothing or say you don't know what to say.
- Be an active listener; grieving people need a safe person who will handle them with care.
- Be present: your presence is worth more than your words.

Helpful ways to respond to well-intentioned people who say dumb things

🌴 Recognize that in your deep grief and vulnerability you do not need to or will not likely know how to respond to the *well-intentioned* but DUMB comments.

🌴 Recognize that you don't need to internalize the hurtful comments or ruminate over them.

🌴 Recognize that people don't know what to say to you; you are not the problem!

🌴 Recognize that you are free to discard the 'helpful' suggestions that hurt.

🌴 Recognize that people are often uncomfortable with death; ignore the hurtful comments.

🌴 Recognize that in your grief you do not have to respond to *well-intentioned* but DUMB comments.

🌴 Recognize who your trusted friends are; reach out to talk with one in order to debrief.

Love doesn't die with death. Love is like liquid; when it pours out, it seeps into other's lives. Love changes form and shape. Love gets into everything. Death doesn't conquer all; love does. Love wins every single time. Love wins by lasting through death. Love winds by loving more, loving again, loving without fear.

Kate O'Neill

Final Thoughts

Dear Friend

Thank you for taking the time to read this book and showing an interest in the journey of grief, which impacts us all in many ways. Whether you are one who is grieving or wanting to comfort another on their grief journey, I trust this book has been encouraging and you have gleaned helpful insights.

My hope for this book is that it will serve as a resource that can be continually revisited. I want people to understand their own grief as well as the grief of those you care about.

Your comments and suggestions are always welcome, so feel free to contact me at:

well.intentioned.people@gmail.com

Need to purchase more copies? Place your order with me at the above e-mail address or at Lulu.com, Amazon.ca or Amazon.com.

Remember, you are not alone!

NOTES

Books and Articles Worth Noting

Please note this is not an exhaustive list and should not take the place of seeking professional assistance.

Alexander, V. (1991). *Words I never thought to speak.* TO: MacMillan Canada.

Attig, T. (1996). *How we grieve: Relearning the world.* TO: Oxford University Press.

Barber, C. J., & Aspenleiter, S. (1987). *Through the valley of tears.* NJ: Revell.

Bernstein, J. R. (1997). *When the bough breaks.* Kansas City, MO: Andrews McMeel.

Billheimer, P. E. (1977). *Don't waste your sorrows.* MN: Bethany House.

Burr, P. (2006). *Loss, trauma and resilience.* NY: Norton.

Coates, M. (1984). *Silent farewell.* Burlington, ON: Welch.

Corr, C. A., Nabe, C. M., & Corr, D. M. (2000). *Death and dying: Life and living.* CA: Wadsworth.

Doka, K. J. (2016). *Grief is a journey: Finding your path through loss.* TO: Atria Books.

Doka, K. J. (Ed.). (1989). *Disenfranchised grief.* TO: MacMillan Canada.

Doka, K. J. (Ed.). (1996). *Living with grief after sudden loss: Suicide, homicide, accident, heart attack, stroke.*NY: Routledge.

Doka, K. J. (Ed.). (2002). *Disenfranchised grief.* IL: Research Press.

Doka, K. J., & Davidson, J. D. (Eds.). (1998). *Living with grief.* Washington: Brunner.

Doka, K. J., & Martin, T. L. (2010). *Grieving beyond gender.* (Rev. ed.). NY: Taylor & Francis Group.

Fitzgerald, H. (1992). *The grieving child.* TO: Simon & Schuster.

Fanos, J. H. (1996). *Sibling loss.* NJ: Erlbaum.

Grollman, E. (1995). *Bereaved child and teens.* Boston: Beacon Press.

Grollman, E. (1997). *Living when a loved one dies.* Boston: Beacon Press.

Hendricks, W. (2005). *The light that never dies.* Chicago: Northfield.

Hoy, W. G. (2008). *Road to Emmaus: Pastoral care with the dying and bereaved.* Dallas, Texas: Compass Press.

Hoy, W. G. (2015). From strange to typical. *Grief Connect Inc.*

Lewis, C. S. (1961). *A grief observed.* NY: Waller.

Levine, S. (2005). *Unattended sorrow.* NY: Holtzbrinck.

Martin, J. D, (1992). *I can't stop crying.* NY: Key Porter.

Martin, T. L., & Doka, K. J. (2000). *Men don't… cry women do.* NY: Routledge.

Munday, J. (1995). *Surviving the death of a child.* Kentucky: John Knox.

Neimeyer, R. A. (2006). *Lessons of Loss.* TN: Centre of the Study of Loss and Transition.

Neimeyer, R. A. (2011). *Grief and bereavement and contemporary society.* NY: Routledge.

Nouwen, H. J. (1982). *A letter of consolation.* TO: Harper.

O'Rourke, M. (2010). *Befriending death.* NY: Orbis.

Papadatou, D., & Papadatos, C. (Eds.). (1991). *Children and death.* NY: Hemisphere.

Perinatal Services Ontario. (n.d.). *Perinatal grief: Support for men and women.* ON: Canada.

Pearlman, L. A., Wortman, C. B., Feuer, C. A., Farber, C. H., & Rando, T. A. (2014). *Treating traumatic bereavement: A practitioner's guide.* NY: Guilford.

Quinnet, P. G. (1993). *Suicide: The forever decision.* NY: Guildford.

Rando, T. A. (1986). *Grief, dying and death: Clinical interventions for caregivers.* Chicago: Research Press.

Rando, T. A. (Ed.). (1986). *Parental loss of a child.* Chicago: Research Press.

Robinson, R. (2001). *Survivors of suicide.* NY: Career Press.

Sittser, J. (1995). *A grace disguised.* NY: Zondervan.

Smith, H. I. (1994). *On grieving the death of a father.* MN: Augsburg Books.

Smith, H. I. (2001). *When your people are grieving.* Kanas City, MO: Beacon Hill.

Smith, H. I. (2004) *Grievers ask.* MN: Augsburg Books.

Stroebe, M.S., & Schut, H. (1999). The dual process model of coping with bereavement: Rationale and description. *Death Studies, 23,* 197-224.

White, M. A. (1995). *Harsh grief: Gentle hope.* Colorado Springs, CO: Nav Press.

Wolfelt, A. D. (2003). *Understanding your grief: Ten essential touchstones for finding hope and healing your heart.* CO: Companion Press.

Wolfelt, A. D. (2006*). Companioning the bereaved: A soulful guide for counsellors and caregivers.* CO: Companion Press.

Wolfelt, A.D. (2007). *Living in the shadow of the ghosts of grief: A guide for life, living and loving.* CO: Companion Press.

Wolfelt, A.D. (2010). *The wilderness of suicide: Finding your way.* CO: Companion Press.

Wolfelt, A.D. (2010). Eight critical questions for mourners: And the answers that will help you heal. CO: Companion Press.

Wolfelt, A.D. (2012). Companioning the dying: A soulful guide for caregivers. CO: Companion Press.

Wolfelt, A.D. (2012). *Loving from the outside in, mourning from the inside out.* CO: Companion Press.

Wolfelt, A. D. (2014). *The depression of grief: Coping with your sadness and knowing when to get help.* CO: Companion Press.

Wolfelt, A.D. (2015). *The paradoxes of mourning: Healing your grief with three forgotten truths.* CO: Companion Press.

Wolterstorff, N. (1987). *Lament for a son.* Grand Rapids, Michigan: Eerdmans.

Worden, J. W. (2009). *Grief counseling and grief therapy: A handbook for the mental health practictioner.* (4th ed.). NY: Springer.

Wrobleski, A. (1995). (1995). *Suicide: Why?* (2nd ed.). MN: Afterwords.

Yancey, P. (1977). *Where is God when it hurts?* Grand Rapids, Michigan: Zondervan.

Ziglar, Z. (1998). *Confessions of a grieving Christian.* Thomas Nelson.